# Cropping

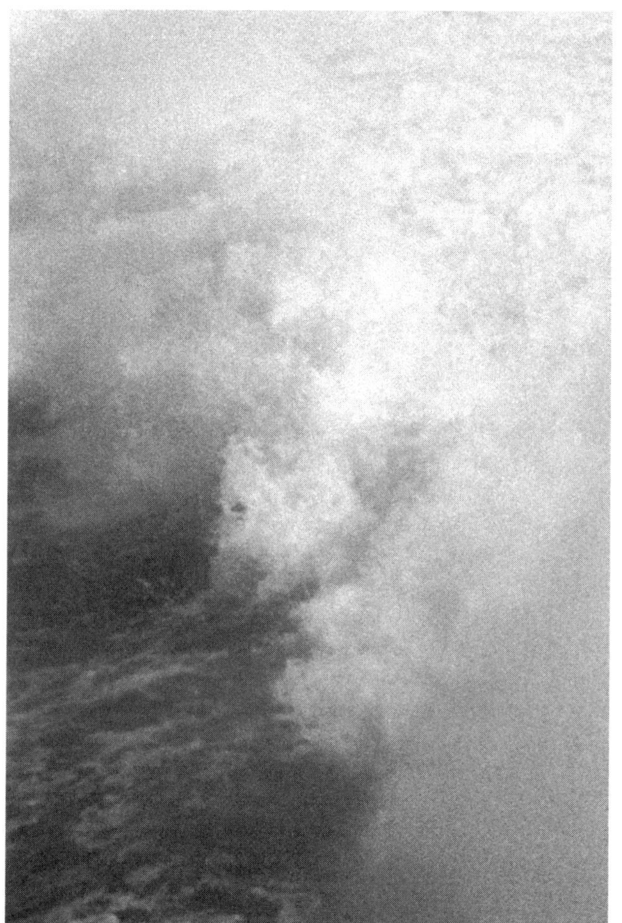

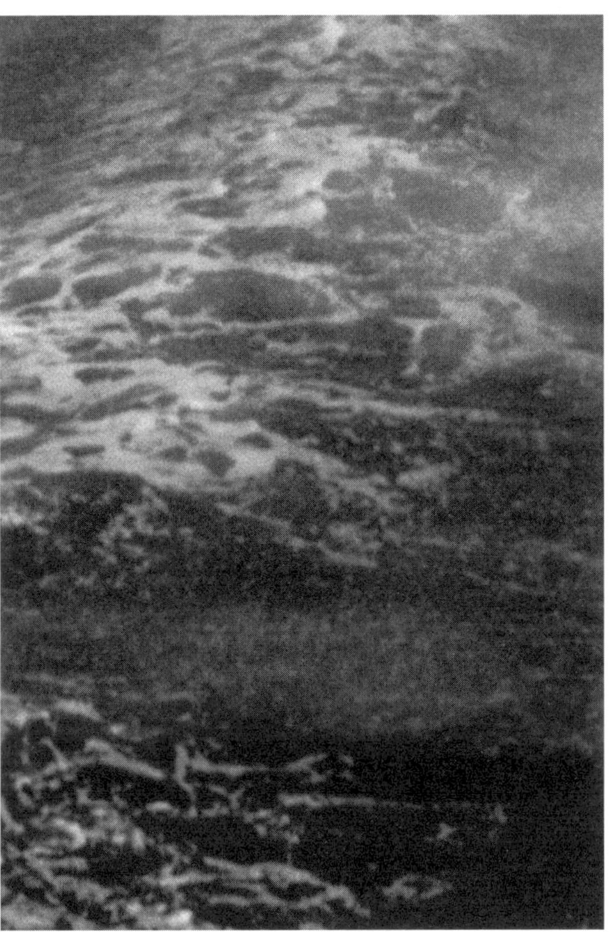

# the Ocean

Bjarne Bare

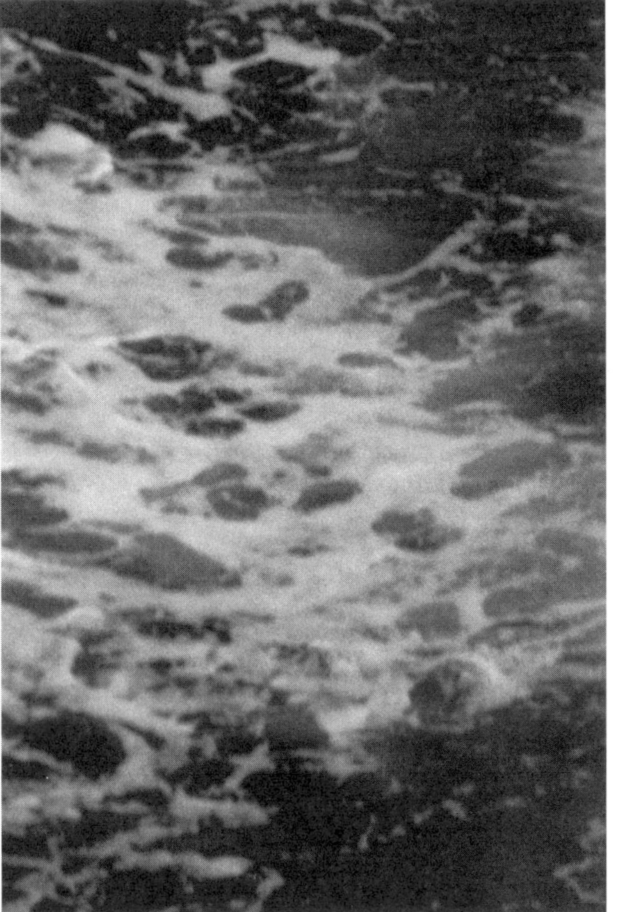

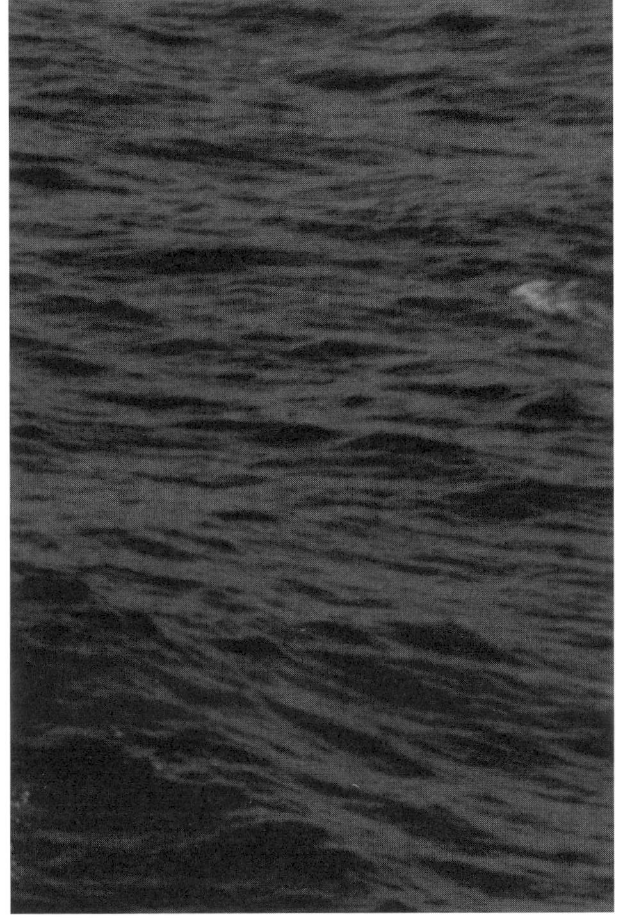

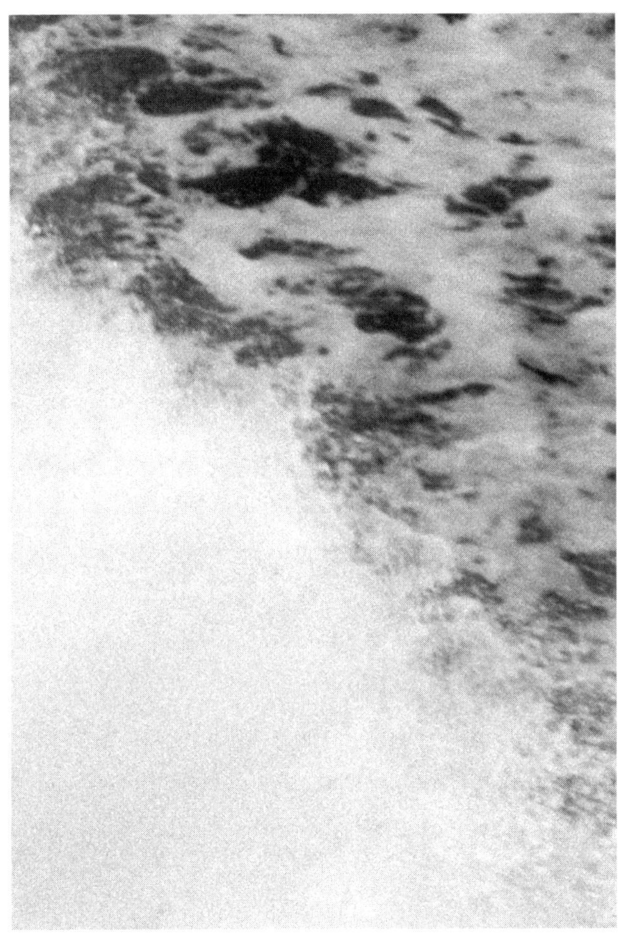

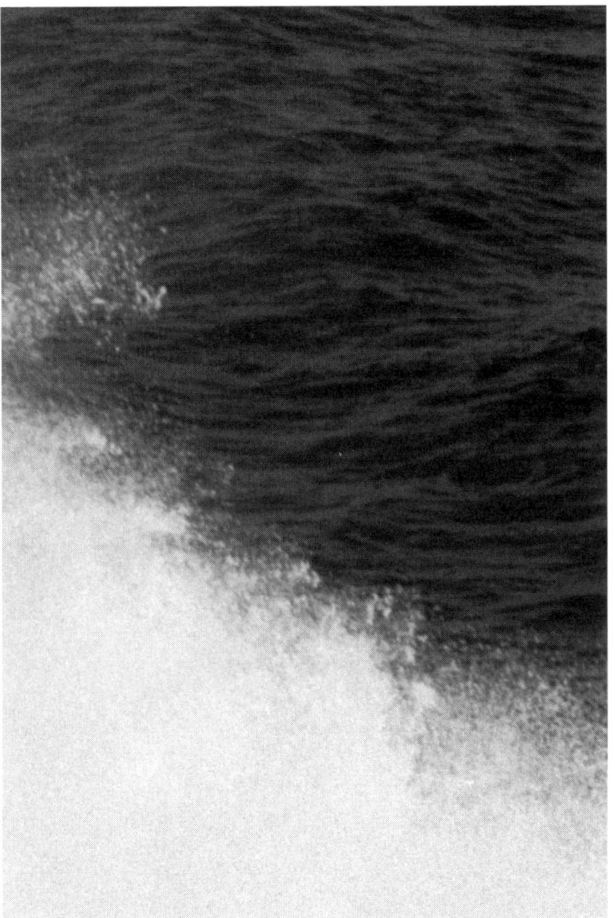

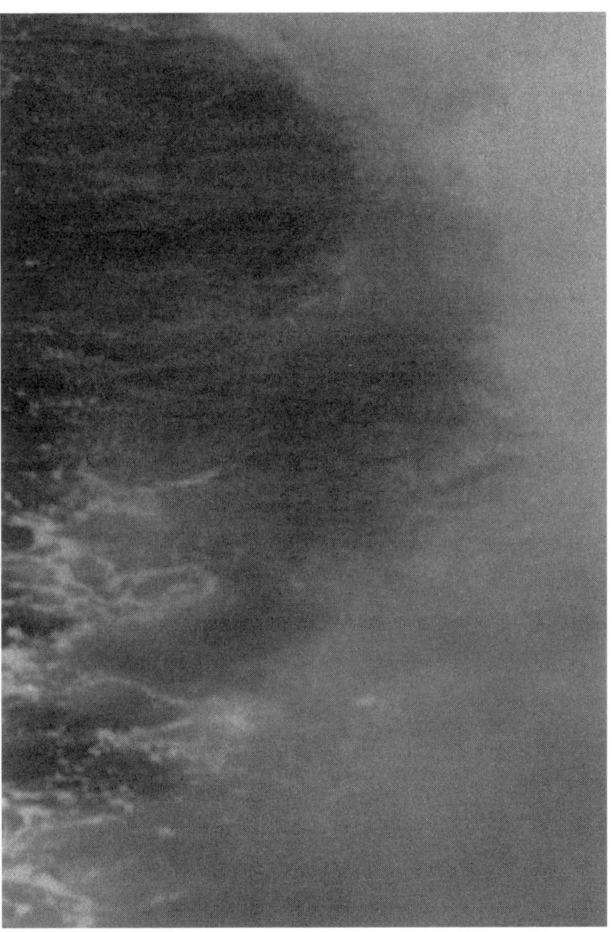

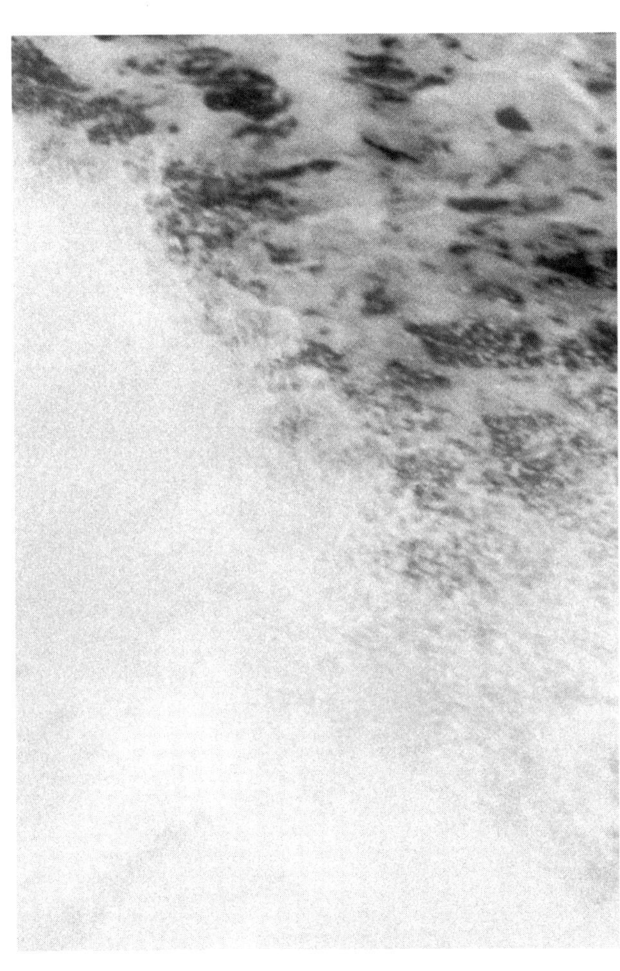

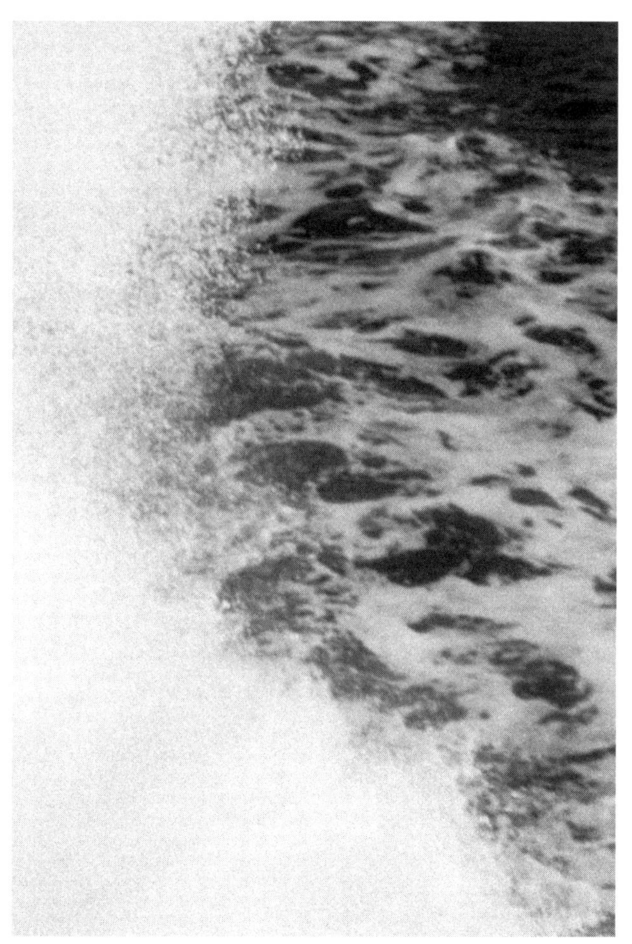

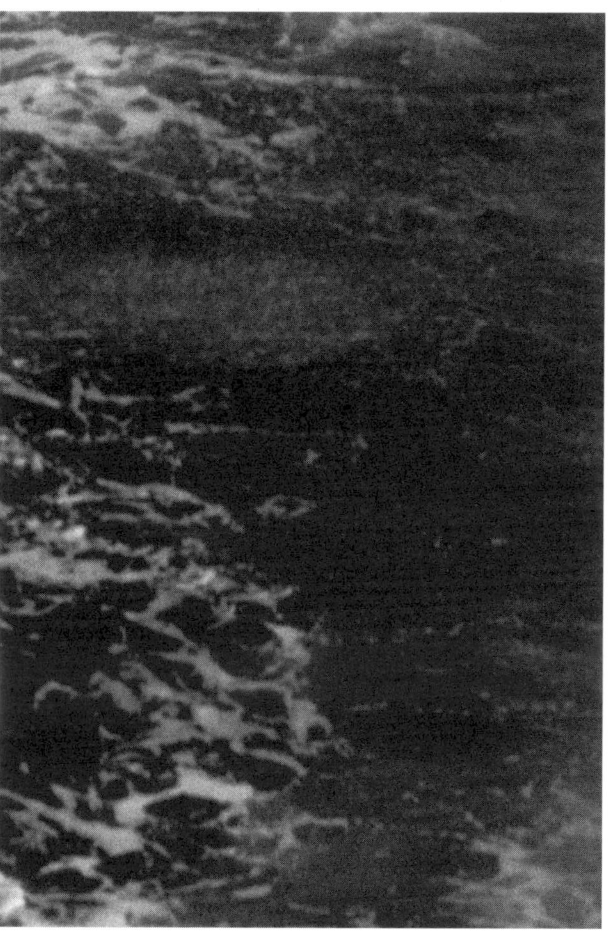

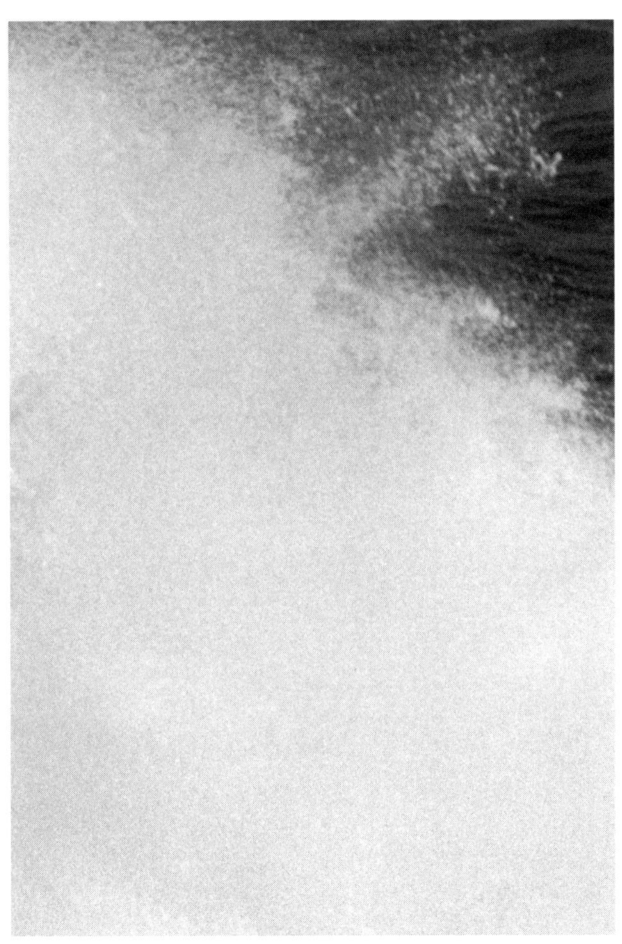

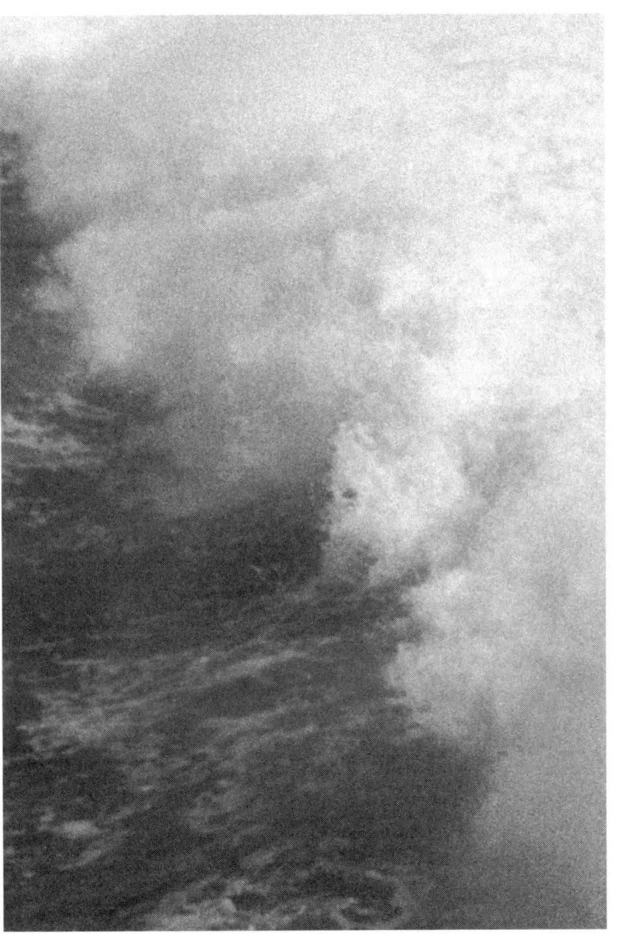

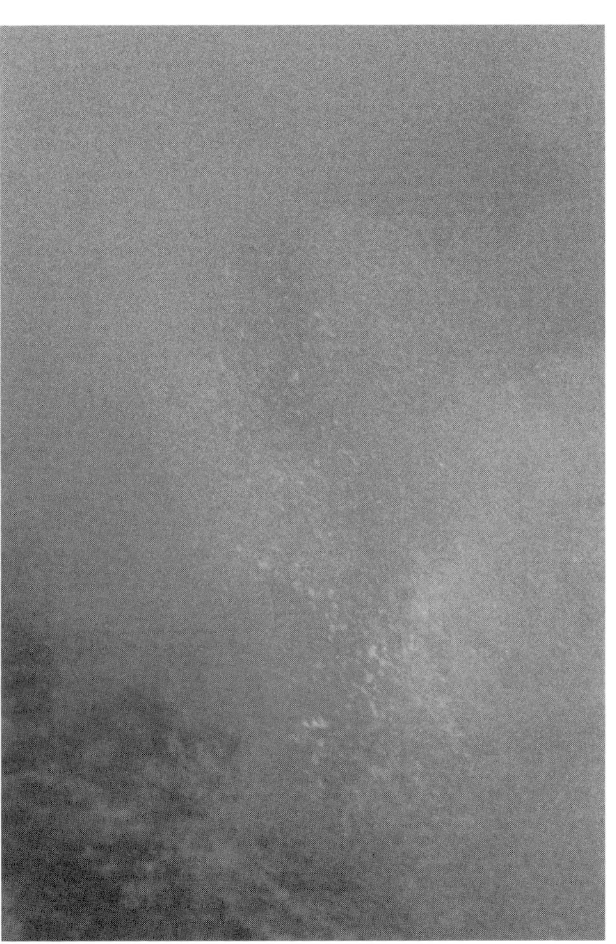

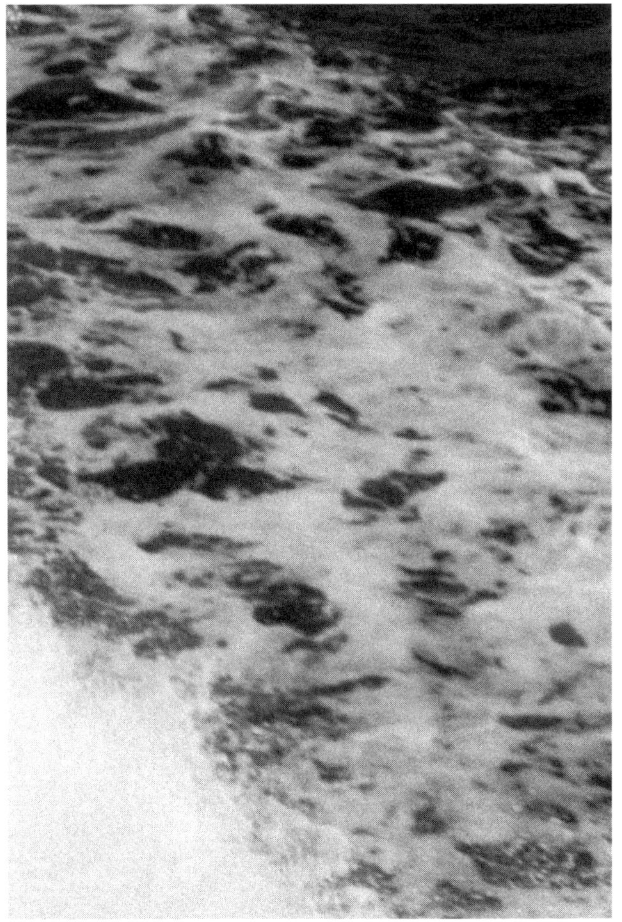

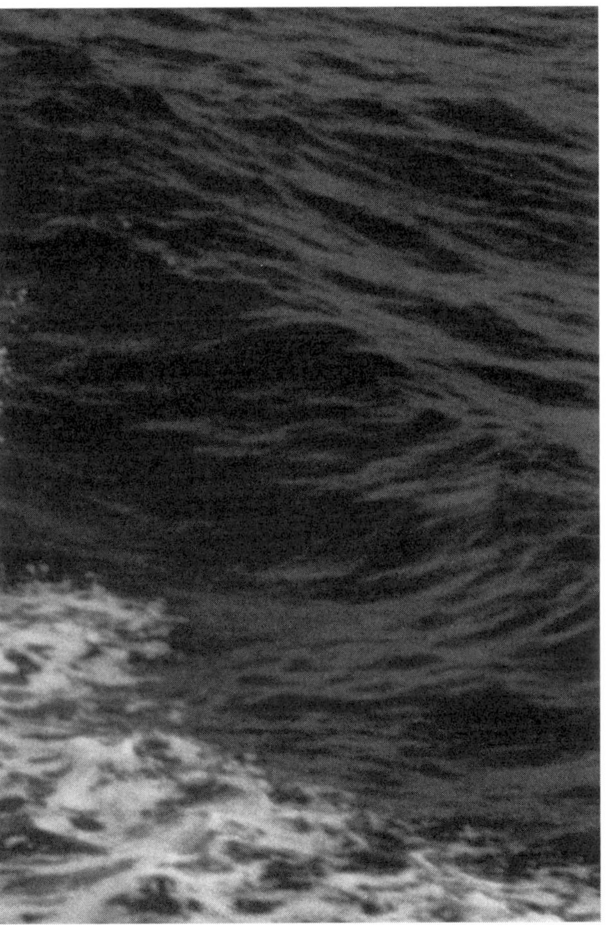

Bjarne Bare

CROPPING
THE OCEAN

Published in 2014 by
Cornerkiosk press, Oslo

ISBN 978-82-998640-5-3



Printed by Tallinn Book Printers

Design by René Josdal & Jens Tandberg

Edition of 250 copies

Cornerkiosk press
www.cornerkiosk.net